Disney · PIXAR

TOY STORY

BOOK 8
Long -i

A Fine Idea

Published by Scholastic Inc., *Publishers since 1920*. SCHOLASTIC and associated logos
are trademarks and/or registered trademarks of Scholastic Inc. All rights reserved.

The publisher does not have any control over and does not assume
any responsibility for author or third-party websites or their content.

This book is a work of fiction. Names, characters, places, and incidents are either the product of the
author's imagination or are used fictitiously, and any resemblance to actual persons, living or dead,
business establishments, events, or locales is entirely coincidental.

ISBN: 978-1-338-57291-9

10 9 8 7 6 5 4 3 2 1   19 20 21 22 23

Printed in Malaysia   106

First printing, 2019

Book design by Marissa Asuncion

Scholastic Inc.

When Andy's toys
come to **life**,
it is **time** to have fun!

What do the toys
like to do?

Rex **likes** to build dinosaur jungles.

That is a **fine idea**!

Wheezy **likes** to **drive** the RC car.

That is a **fine idea**!

Buzz **likes** to play laser tag.
He **shines** a **bright light**.

Now Woody is "it"!
That is a **fine idea**!

Woody **likes** to play rodeo.

That is a **fine idea**!

Jessie **likes** to play volleyball.

That is a **fine idea**!

Bo Peep **likes** to play **hide**-and-seek.

That is a **fine idea**.

But the most fun **time**,
the **time** the toys **like** best,
is playing with Andy and
his friends.

Now, that is a **fine idea**!